DOODLES OF A SURVIVOR: MY JOURNEY TO JAMES

JAMES E. ANDERSON JR.

Copyright © 2021 by James E. Anderson Jr. An *Imprint* of Journal Joy Publishers

All rights reserved. Printed in the United States of America. No part of this book may be reproduced, distributed, or transmitted in any form or by any means, without the prior written permission of the authors, except in the case of brief quotations embodied in critical reviews and certain other noncommercial uses permitted by copyright law.

For information on publishing, contact Journal Joy at Info@thejournaljoy.com. www.thejournaljoy.com

ISBN: 978-1-957751-00-9

Edited by: Nicole Gyimah

First paperback edition, 2022

DEDICATED TO LIFE AND ALL ITS LESSONS

DOODLES OF A SURVIVOR: MY JOURNEY TO JAMES

Several unsuccessful relationships (platonic, familial, and romantic) lead me to write this book.

I started to write out stories of all the perceived wrongs done to me. Detailing the incidents for my readers to be empathetic for all the horrible experiences I had. Trust me many were traumatic. I had reason to feel wronged and taken advantage of. Through my own examination, I learned information, while ascertaining some of it from those who weren't supposed to tell me. I was ready to lay out my facts in black and white, and almost did so anonymously to avoid ruffling any feathers with my T.R.U.T.H. I was diagnosing people, labeling them with titles that made sense to me. This was going to be my tell-all book answering questions for some, yet serving as a voice to individuals with similar experiences...

What I now understand is that my motive was much different. I muddled around for two years developing "HE TOO" – the original title of this piece - taking advantage of all the publicity around the #METOO movement. This was to be a book about the underreported and swept under the rug phenomenon of emotional, physiological, and physical abuse committed against men. I was being motivated to tell my story to receive empathy, hoping to be viewed differently from how I thought people saw me. The shame of multiple failed marriages which didn't end well had me walking around like I had an Unlovable / Unable to Love tattoo on my forehead. Guilt-based behavior never leads to a good end. At the time I knew I needed to shift my motivation from trying to overcome the humiliation.

Somewhere along the healing journey, talking about these things no longer felt healthy but like I was waking up every day replaying the traumatic experiences of abuse, abandonment, and betrayal. I was writing and editing these experiences signaling to my body that we were PRESENTLY in these fight or flight scenarios. Imagine that ... choosing daily to put my mind and body through torment and calling it part of the healing process.

I wrote for a couple of years on and off and it became much more off when I noticed myself feeling better when I didn't give my writing that much attention. The premise of what you think/talk about grows started to guide me.

I knew I wanted to continue to write and share but not in such an out of control, I had no power over these experiences' way. There was a time for that, and it had served its purpose in my healing process. I desired to share in a way that acknowledges my experience but doesn't leave it there. I'm not here to be a whistleblower. I wanted to speak to people in a real way that inspires people to get up no matter how many times they get knocked down. Even acknowledging that I had something to do with me being down here.

#HETOO has evolved into this collection of Word Art - thoughts, poems, and short stories which birthed the first iteration of what came to be known to my Facebook followers as "Doodles Of A Survivor".

These entries grew out of my thought processes while working through being diagnosed with Multiple Myeloma - a deadly blood cancer. I decided early on in this diagnosis that I wasn't going to treat it traditionally (in my response to the diagnosis, in my treatment of it, and not to be afraid of it - hence dying). I could be working, walking, driving, on a plane, or watching television when I would just get inspired to share whatever was prevalent in my thoughts at the time. As there was no single format as these thoughts and emotions came to me, some read as poems, some as a social media post, and others as diary entries. I hope that you are entertained, inspired, and led to Self-Reflection and Self-Love through the sharing of my thoughts as I work to get back to James.

CONTENTS

Volume 1: My Friend Cancer 1

Volume 2: Let It Burn 4

Volume 3: Behavior Is More Truthful Than Words 7

Volume 4: 21 Questions? 10

Volume 5: Skin Tone 12

Volume 6: Dandelion 14

Volume 7: Dear Daddy 16

Volume 8: Another Sleepless Night 21

Volume 9: Sexual Seduction 23

Volume 10: Who Shot Ya? 25

Volume 11: Hold My Hand 27

Volume 12: Victorious Secret 30

Volume 13: The Loop 31

Volume 14: Obituary 33

Volume 15: Man Up 36

Volume 16: Self-Suffering 38

Volume 17: Spades 40

Volume 18: Seeds Planted 42

Volume 19: Vibrational Creation 45

Volume 20: You Don't Know Me 48

Volume 21: Talk To Me Nice 50

Volume 22: Parenting 101 51

Volume 23: Funeral Arrangements 53

Volume 24: Chemotherapy Is Like Ether 55

Volume 25: Money Not The Answer 57

Volume 26: A Face Full Of Tears 58

Volume 27: If I Die Today 59

Volume 28: Cancer - Still My Friend 61

Volume 29: Breathe Again 63

Volume 30: Fear Factor 65

Volume 31: Denver 67

Volume 32: Imagination 69

Volume 33: Your Peoples 71

Volume 34: Unbreakable 72

Volume 35: Handlebars 75

Volume 36: Selfish 77

Volume 37: Blind Spots-Handlebars 2 78

Volume 38: Pandemic Thoughts 81

Volume 39: Self Love / Algorithms 83

Volume 40: Soleil 85

Volume 41: Protecting My Peace 90

Volume 42: Fall Semester 1990 92

In Closing 94

VOLUME 1

MY FRIEND CANCER

I decided today. To embrace this Cancerous thing happening in my body

It's hardly a new decision though.
I have been making it daily.
Since June 2015 when I got the diagnosis.

Your body is attacking itself sir.

It's Cancer sir.
Numbly responded.......Word???
Replied sir you got the right one If you need one.
To show one.
How to be a real one.
In the face of uncertain outcomes, No asking how Come

What's to fear? I'm God's son!!!

I will keep this smile.
I will keep living my life.
If it's seven days or seven thousand.

I am not trying to waste one.

I'm embracing my friend cancer.

To hate it, I would have to hate myself.

In addition, I'm loving myself more than ever since this diagnosis.

Cancer is a GREAT TEACHER and I'm embracing it for all the lessons it has taught me.

Most I didn't ask to learn and would have preferred not to.

If you have had to encounter my friend
You may be afraid because most people talk badly about him
But he's taught me lessons on loyalty, trust, forgiveness, gratitude, and attitude.
Sure, he's a friend that you don't want to overstay their welcome
And I'm trying everything to kindly escort him from my house/body.
But while he's here, I plan to teach him some things.
I accept you cancer and appreciate all that you have come to show me.
I know you're shocked because most people hate you.
But I don't hate you as much as I don't want you in my body.
I'M GOING TO LOVE YOU TO DEATH.

Every Smile

James E. Anderson Jr

Every warm embrace

Every encounter you have with me

My friend is there too

Often shaping the interaction

He reminds me this may be my last time in this space with this person so enjoy it.

This may be your last conversation with this person.

Make it a good one.

In my imperfections

I don't always get it 100 percent

I'm Learning 100 percent perfection was never the goal.

But my friend gently reminds me and gives me another chance tomorrow …so far.

VOLUME 2

LET IT BURN

How about just throwing caution to the wind and letting it all go.

Do I want to leave this physical presence on a high of just living without fear or care for what others think?

On a bucket list mission of sorts devoid of parameters or morality.

Just unadulterated wilding!

If I'm going, why not go partying like A rock star?

The Nature to be such a person had to be in you, to begin with, and I have never been a quitter.

Yes, I have quit but that doesn't make me a quitter.

Sure, I'm faced with immeasurable odds.

I'm going to face it with immeasurable force.

Chemo and all its cousins had their chance to bring order to the situation.

I just wanted to live, and docs said this gives me a better chance of survival so poison me now if you must save me later.

Wait …. amid mental anguish and emotional turmoil, one's miseducation (i.e., Ignorance) can easily be played on Even if innocently and with good intent.

I mean in plain English, what Medical Field Professionals are saying is the best option we have is to poison you. They are going to put enough poison in me to kill the disease (hopefully) and not enough that it kills me and my healthy organs (hopefully)

If not given any other options, we do what millions of cancer patients before me (many who have died from their disease) used as their primary treatment plan. Poison.

How about we need an army of modalities to address the many forms and strands differently.

I am inclusive and in favor of: Pharmaceutical companies, Research Institutions, Holistic and Diet Based Therapy, Mindfulness, Meditation, and anything else that is helpful to the patient.

Cancer, Leukemia, Myeloma I'm waging a war against you and through the process of your eradication I will become so much stronger, compassionate, loving, accepting, and more prepared to stand and give my testimony. A testimony of inspiration. A testimony of faith. A testimony that outlives me in its impact. A testimony that gives God Glory.

I'm fighting for my physical body, my mental awareness and stability, and my emotional maturity. At some point, I won't be able to sustain all three. Until that day I wage war against anything that comes against my physical, mental, or emotional health.

If we all looked at life like this there might be less cancer in the world. Let this be my message of legacy:

Fight for your Physical, Mental, and Emotional Health Daily ....For Your Life Depends on It

One Day I want it read:

Here lies a humble soldier who fought with everything he had while living life and inspired many. JEA JR.

VOLUME 3

BEHAVIOR IS MORE TRUTHFUL THAN WORDS

Halfway through falling in love I looked up and saw I was falling by myself.

Physically, emotionally, and psychologically I have been abused before.
Maybe I'm sensitive and overstating that I have just been played on occasion.
Nobody forced me. I willingly fell in love and let love hurt me.

Greatest intentions don't always pan out.
No more marriages; I'm just dating.
Until my heart starts feeling like it doesn't have patience. Just a few months ago we were just having relations.

Now I have thoughts of us being upgraded.
You got my heart racing. This feels so amazing.
But every day I get more into you, you seem more complacent.
I'm loving you and letting you in places I swore no one could go again.
What makes it hurt worse, is when reciprocation isn't as strong.

Searching for someone that I can talk to, trust with my heart, and believe in.

Not another unhealed one committing treason.

I'm trying to love again......Please be the reason.

When I settle down, I'm all in. You had me believing in the possibility of you and me.

Until the disrespect started to creep in.

I need a sister that sees my wounds and scars and helps heal them. A sister that protects my heart and puts me first.

When I'm down you are my comedian.

When I'm sick, you're my nurse.

I thought you were the one for me to try to love again.

Then day by day, it seemed you were less and less interested. Yeah, shit hurts.

Yeah, I'm accountable and responsible for my behavior.

Yeah, Yeah, Yeah. I'm tired though.

I'm not up to investigating to find out why.

It is what it is and the why is not as important as the why not.

Why not understand it's just another dream deferring moment?

Maybe I'm just a great friend, not meant to be tied to one person in love.

Maybe I just need to be so in love with myself that there isn't space for anyone else.

I thought I was in a space where only someone that came absolutely correct would be let in.

Now look at me.

Confused, Conflicted, and Cast Away.

I gave it my all……put my best foot forward in the face of a tough ride ahead and woke up one day feeling like it's not enough to get back what I want and need. No matter what I give of myself, the truth won't change anything. If someone isn't feeling you at the same level, (for whatever reason), regardless of what you do, they still are not going to feel you outside of where they do. Words may say different things, but Behavior is more truthful than words.

VOLUME 4

21 QUESTIONS?

After settling in with my diagnosis, I came to Total Peace.

Then the questions began... Some in my head and some from the mouths of others.

(In my Biggie Voice)
When the chemo's in the system
Ain't no telling if the next step is radiation
Why are we cooking cancer patients?
Are people going to treat me differently? It's Cancer not Syphilis. One Year after I'm gone, will they just forget or will they reminisce?

Is this pity, attention, or genuine?
Do people really pray for me when they say they do?

Why Me?
Who is in my same position and afraid to talk about it? Can I really do all things through Christ?

How are you so strong?

How many people are going to be at my funeral (not that it's ANYTIME soon?)

When is my hair going to fall out?

Why am I so happy?

Should you be out in the rain? What?????????

I see you traveling. You trying to live life up before...?

Why are we not curing diseases after all this time?

With all this technology, why can't I get one on Amazon Prime?

Why are people still ashamed to get mental therapy?

How is it legal to sell food that's killing people?

We avoid toxic people.

Why do we consume toxic man-made food?

Why you Doodling?

Is this a cry for attention? NOOOOO

VOLUME 5

SKIN TONE

If you haven't seen the movie Queen and Slim, I recommend you do. This movie touches on so many topics directly and indirectly. The thing that resonated with me was something I have dealt with from a very young age. SKIN TONE. Being a dark-skinned person has been tough because society starts to implant in your head that not only are you a minority that's seen as less than by many, but you are at the bottom of the totem pole in that category also. Terms like "Blackie", "Tar Baby", "Spook" and more became terms that cut to my core. I became ashamed of something that I should have taken pride in. It shouldn't have taken anything outside of me to help me feel good about me and anything in my physical make up.

I was embarrassed in high school when I was called Shaka Zulu by a classmate. Today I would take that same moniker as a compliment. I'm being compared to a warrior, soldier, and legend. Yet, I still have moments when I walk into a room and think about these people are looking at my skin and making a judgment or see a picture of myself and think. "I'm too dark in that picture".

The mental anguish and self-sabotage caused by issues around skin is under addressed and unappreciated by those that don't experience the traumatic effects of it. It was great to see two heavily melanin lead characters represent on the big screen. I cried several times in the theater.

For many reasons

VOLUME 6

DANDELION

Is it a flower?

Is it a weed?

When you look at a well-manicured lawn and see that one yellow spot emerging in the center.

Do you want to cut it before seeing just what it can become? Or do you water it and see how it may add to the overall landscape?

Sometimes our picture of perfection is persistently pushed to the limits of societal BS.

Why not have a lawn full of dandelions if that's your pleasure?

When looking out the window, am I concerned with how I feel about my lawn or what my neighbors think about it. Maybe someone else's eyesore is the most beautiful peace granting blessings for you.

The universe won't always package a blessing the way we might have thought. Again, Societal BS often reinforced by the irrationality of chasing the Jones's Versus chasing one's own dreams and aspirations.

Find your dandelion.

Water it.

Multiply it.

Keep your admiration of dandelions to yourself if that's best for your mental health and peace. But don't deny yourself that joy.

For the sake of keeping someone else comfortable.

VOLUME 7

DEAR DADDY

What you know about not seeing your father for 8 years?

Then he shows up in the middle of the night when you are 15 years old on his deathbed.

Let me paint the picture:
Late night, room door closed, watching TV.
Probably Three's Company
Then mom knocks on the door saying "You've Got Company"

Walk in the living room.
Guess who I saw?
Pops... the man I hadn't seen in 8 years.
Dad.... then I went numb. No smile, no tears
My dad wasn't recognizable, and it wasn't from age. I think years of drug abuse had exposed him to AIDS.

Over the past 8 years, I often heard I'm just like you.

Looking at you now, I'm not sure to pity you or spite you.
I mean what do you know about being on the court thinking you are the man.
On the free-throw line.

Take a pause and look in the stands.
It's full of people but their fans are not my fam.
Damn it Dad!
I wanted you there.
I wanted your cheer.
I wanted to drive home with you after a win or a loss.

Then sit in the driveway for 30 minutes hearing what I did wrong.

I forgave you; understanding that addiction is a hard knock on the psyche.
No one knows I played every high school game with your obituary in my Nikes.
I wish I remembered ANYTHING that was said that night Dad.
But what's most important is that before you left, you remembered ME Dad.
Not even having the strength to walk on your own Dad, You had a friend bring you from Harlem to Newark in a cab.

You could have been too embarrassed for me to see you like this. No ego, no pride.

The most loving thing you ever did.
Taught me to stand up and be a man accepting responsibility and the consequences of my behavior.
So, there isn't any hatred for you.
You taught me accountability.

So, moving forward, what do I do?

Accept Responsibility.

Yani ran track, Jah played ball, SaVonne danced and spoke. I was there for it all.

As a result, the positivity of your legacy, is my never wavering presence.

In the lives of three,

I know the trauma of an absent father and committed early that this curse would go no further. All the events I wanted you to be at Dad.

I did that Dad... I was that Dad.

For me and for you, we did that Dad.

Don't know if I ever said Thank You.

Don't remember ever saying I Love You.

Don't know if you think you are forgiven.

Dad. Thank You! I LOVE YOU! I Forgive You!

Parental absence by choice, death, or otherwise, traumatizes a child. If you are alive, be a parent to your child. If you can, be a parent figure to someone else's child. Children need more love than we think. Love isn't buying Jordans and iPhones. Real love gets a child in therapy if need be. Furthermore, there are a lot of adult bodies being run by hurting children inside.

Love them too.

I talk to little James from time to time and parent him in the ways I missed as a youngster. Nothing against Agnes

Anderson. My Momma, whose parents couldn't read, held it down as a single parent greatly assisted by my big sister Sandra Carlton.

Agnes, James Edward Sr, Sandra Anderson (Carlton), and James Jr (me)

Daddy,

There are so many people in the world who grow up not knowing their dads. Luckily, you haven't made me one of those people. I am grateful to have you in my life, even though we haven't always gotten along. I am happy that we have gotten so much closer and have a better relationship. You are someone that I can depend on to always be there for me, and I thank you so much for that. After Mommy died, I didn't know if I could go on with just one parent. Your love and sacrifice made it so much easier for me to go through her death and go on with just a dad — a great dad. I LOVE YOU!

YaYa

Written by SaVonne Da Sawndra Anderson

James, and SaVonne Anderson

VOLUME 8

ANOTHER SLEEPLESS NIGHT

Another night without sleep.

Guess my brain is too full during the day to give thought to these things.

It doesn't make sense because I think about them throughout the day too.

But sometimes at night, I can't shut it down.

2am is becoming the norm.

Often falling asleep when the sun comes up.

The problem is not just that I'm not getting enough sleep.

It's these late hours when the demons defeated from the past show up.

I mean I'm awake; I guess I'll do something with the time. Grab the laptop and be productive.

Out of nowhere comes lustful thoughts.

Close that up, put on the tv that should make me sleepy. Two hours later, I've watched four episodes of Judge Judy.

All the while these thoughts won't let me rest. I'm overdosing on melatonin.

And I'm wide awake.

So many thoughts, decisions, and trials for one man to face. After months, I have surrendered.

I know I got to do something.

Do something with my thoughts.

Make the decisions I am avoiding.

Face every trial head on.

AND GET SOME SLEEP.

Goodnight

VOLUME 9

SEXUAL SEDUCTION

I used selfish means to get the drawers of Queens.

Not thinking of the consequences of carnal deeds.

Because sex became the source of my self-esteem. I knew John 3:16.

But had three notches on the belt by the age of 16. In the hood, you are taught to get it by any means. But not about abortions, STDS, and unwanted pregnancies. In Volume 7 I shared I had no pops in my house.

So, friends putting my manhood in doubt was tantamount.

To being unaccepted by yet another group.

So, I'm hell-bent on getting their approval.

Even if it meant letting them smell my fingers.

After an episode with Lil Bonita,

Thank God, She Put Me On.

Every action has a reaction and my ignorance had a cost.

See, I woke up one-night private parts ablaze.

Just yesterday sex was a fun phase.

Where are my friends now?

Who can tell me how?

To cool this burning happening in my Lee Jeans.

Hit the phone book and made an appointment at 110 William Street. Steel instruments stuck in tender places.

Given two weeks of pills and told don't eat dairy.

Exposure to sexual themes, under-reported molestation, sexual abuse, training youth to keep "secrets", shaming, and not believing those that do find the courage to speak up, can have an impact on the youth long term. If you've never spoken up, speak up, even if it's only to heal yourself.

VOLUME 10

WHO SHOT YA?

Who Shot Ya?

Cancer, Narcissistic Abuse, or Childhood Trauma.

All these things have been my experience.
Some might use these truths as a reason to be dishonest, disrespectful, or as justification for being hurtful to others.
I choose to just keep loving.
Even when loving you is killing me.
Sounds like a noble idea.
But how many scars can one take for the team?
When others are playing one on one.
If I'm looking out for you and you are looking out for you, one of us is making a bad decision.
Might be me if I keep making these choices repeatedly.
Love thy neighbor is what I've been taught, forgive seventy times; seventy is what God says.
Yet, my human mind is starting to operate from self-preservation and give people one shot to be disrespectful and unloving.

Sure, correct, and watch for corrected behavior.

If promised change is not adhered to, then you know what to do. Self-preservation must be more powerful than Love for others. Put your mask on first.

Otherwise, you roll the dice on being a victim or a Survivor.

VOLUME 11

HOLD MY HAND

Sometimes I want someone to hold my hand.

Sometimes I want someone to put one of my shoes on and walk with me.

Sometimes I want to talk about it and sometimes I want to ignore it

Sometimes I sit in waiting rooms wanting someone to kick it with during the wait.

Sometimes I enjoy being alone because I have surrounded myself with people so much during this lifetime.

But I must carry my own cross without any expectation of support.

Although, I am fully aware of the army of people willing to show up and support me (THANK YOU).

Cancer alters your emotions and reality for the better and possibly the worst.

So many decisions to make treatment plans, disclosing to people, attending support groups, people to trust, insurance implications, who will be my caregivers.

Sometimes I want someone to help me make these decisions. But cancer has also taught me that this is my life, and I must live or die with it and these choices.

While they may be difference makers and should be made with some input from others,

This will ultimately affect ME the most.

I shouldn't have relied on Cancer to come to this life understanding.

Yet, I am grateful that I was taken here. I am trying to make decisions about the totality of my life.

The person most affected by my choices and decisions will be Me.

That doesn't stop my desire to sometimes have my hand held.

This morning, as I sit on the doctor's examination table and type. I paused for a second.

To Hold My Own Hand.

It doesn't feel as good as the dopamine rush from the support of another right now, but I will get comfortable. For this is the battle of Self-Love, Self-Care, Self-Awareness, and Self Esteem. They all begin and end with Self.

This isn't my cancer battle but my human battle that Cancer has brought to the surface for me to address.

My Friend, My Bro, My A1-Day. With my two hands, I don't do a lot on Facebook, so I really don't know how to comment on your page. With those same two hands, I can remember playing football with you. With those same two hands, I played wiffle ball with you (until the ball went into Mrs. Perkins's yard). With those same two hands, we played Atari together. With those same two hands, we put on boxing gloves and jabbed each other in my backyard and use those same hands to defend each other up until this day. This text was sent to let you know, those same two hands (right/left/or both) are still available if you need to hold on to them.
DOODLES OF A BRO

SALUTE...

Charles "Scooby" Williams

VOLUME 12

VICTORIOUS SECRET

Win Quietly.

Go about the business

Of your business successfully and quietly.

Use Humility as the Fertilizer In Your Victory Garden.

Let your Victories be a Secret.

VOLUME 13

THE LOOP

Being alive for 51 years, it took 48 years to understand I've been living under subconscious

programming. The universe has a way of getting our attention: mine was Cancer. People consider Cancer something you fight against.

I've decided to look at it differently.

What are you here to teach me Cancer?

Response: I'm here to show you all your demons, fears, and unaddressed traumas that have created loops in your life.

Therapy has helped me bring some of these loops to the surface. Repetition Compulsion is the appropriate term for what I've been experiencing. Basically it means, subconsciously doing the same thing over and over. Different faces, but the same characteristics. I've not been able to find what started the loop, but at some point, in my childhood, I experienced something that planted a seed to be the savior of others. As a result, in my intimate life, I've attracted and have been attracted to people that I could save. I've overcommitted too soon and then fought with everything to not be seen as a

loser/quitter by the others; should the relationship end. Over and over my intimate relationships would play out similarly.

What a birthday present to discover! I've been trying to subconsciously close the Loop. This revelation gives me such understanding, peace, and the opportunity to close the Loop independently. No longer allowing the loop to control my decisions. Who can I save anyway....ME? The one that really needs it most.

THANK YOU, Cancer

Love James

VOLUME 14

OBITUARY

This doodle was one of the first written after my Multiple Myeloma Diagnosis in 2015. A few lines were adjusted but it's raw feeling at that time. This took courage to share.

I don't know why I feel like my life is coming to an end. I'm very concerned about dying soon. I don't want to concern my family and friends with these thoughts, but I also don't want to leave and not have folks know how I felt about them and my wishes for them moving forward. Please do not see this as some suicide note. I'm not trying to take my own life.

Kym, I'm sorry this was such a short ride. After waiting so long to get married it seems unfair that we part this soon. I love you and wish the best for you. Continue your path to being truly healed and whole.

SaVonne: You are my first-born child and I have seen you grow into a wonderful woman. Not a perfect woman; but progress is not about perfection. We've talked in the past about the lives of your grandmother, my father, and your mother, and the issues that you need to avoid. I'm concerned about your decision making regarding those choices and I'm prayerful that you will recognize this and do

better. You are too bright, too talented, and too blessed. I am hopeful that you will reach your potential, break the cycle, and make a huge mark on this family and this world. I know you can do it. Adulthood gives you more say over your life but what you do with that responsibility can be costly.

JaVon my son: You have so much potential and have been blessed with the opportunity to develop in every aspect of your life. Yet, your stubborn attitude, lack of commitment, and laziness will let all that opportunity go to waste. I have always watched you waiting for the switch to go on where your commitment, willingness to work hard, and desire would line up with the results you want for yourself. It hasn't happened yet and seeing many people waste talent and opportunity because of bad attitude, being unteachable, and stubbornness. No pain, no gain. I LOVE YOU and patiently wait for your maturity and self-awareness.

I am so proud of the three of you and prayerful that you will continue to grow and not let my departure pull you back or become an excuse for not doing your absolute best. I am asking that each of you step up and don't take any day for granted. Life is too short. I pray that you use me as motivation and not as a crutch. Make me happy and proud. I love you all dearly. I was not a perfect man, and I made many mistakes and bad choices. No part of this was ever done to hurt any of you intentionally.

My mother, sister, lifetime supporters, and molders of me, thank you so much for all you have done to help me become the man I am today. I could have never done any of this without your support, love, lessons, patience, and prayers. The two of you raised a man

without a man in the house and I commend you for keeping me on the straight and narrow while also giving me enough leash to have life experiences to learn from.

Written September 2015 3 months after Cancer Diagnosis

VOLUME 15

MAN UP

Men Lie, Women Lie

Numbers Don't

Sometimes men lie about the fact that we cry
Men's hearts break, men's hearts ache

Surprise .... Men have hearts ladies just been trained that showing them emotions might get you labeled soft

Labels don't just come from guys either, I done heard many ladies making fun of a man who gets emotional.

If you ridicule a man for being in touch with his emotions in a way that puts him in a place to be vulnerable, honest, and unrepressed. You can't then be surprised when that man is secretive, dishonest, and depressed.

Furthermore that "soft" dude is less likely to beat on that head.

No excuse my guys. If you can't be appreciated for your whole self, if you can't share your emotions, fears, and flaws in the safety of a supportive environment...... Spend less time (if any) in that space. That's your responsibility .... doesn't matter if it's friends, family, or a romantic relationship.

I'm now a card-carrying emotion on my sleeve "soft" dude. I'm not afraid to cry publicly or privately. Anything we repress and bury hasn't gone anywhere and I believe causes many of our illnesses. Either directly or through the behaviors (alcohol abuse, overeating, drug abuse, etc.) we use to distract us from them. I'm guilty of it but that's the past. That's real MANNING UP to me.

Man Up Brothers. Get IN your Feelings

VOLUME 16

SELF-SUFFERING

We as humans create our own suffering by thinking that things should be other than how they are!

Look into each tough circumstance in life as a hurdle as a blessing here to teach you something. Don't bury, ignore, or blame. Victim playing is the opposite of growth. Took me a minute to get this one. Oh, what a joy to embrace every life challenge as the teachers that they are. This mindset blesses you individually and promotes an environment to bless humanity because you take full responsibility for whatever comes your way. No blame of others, no questioning God, no self-blame or why Me?.. sincerely sitting with it and seeking the lesson from even the most detrimental circumstances (death, loss of job, home foreclosure, divorce, declining health, sexual assault, etc.).

I have decided to embrace ALL circumstances. I'm Actually starting to seek out the hurdles in life for the lessons.

James E. Anderson Jr

VOLUME 17

SPADES

Life is like a game of spades

When I first learned how to play Spades

I was good when I was dealt a good hand

When I was dealt a less impressive hand I wasn't as confident
Over time the more I played

The more I learned to make a handout of what some might consider a bad hand

The more I played

The more I learned the subtleties of the game (life)

- How to read people's body language
- How to predict what's likely to happen next
- Knowing who I want on my team
- Understanding that people are habitual — they usually repeat their behavior

- Giving off an energy of confidence when the facts say you shouldn't. Always confuses your opponent
- Trusting my intuition (experiences)

Before you say you don't have any books

Take another look at your hand

It still looks bad.

Do the best you can with it and believe the next hand will be better.

When you lose the game (and you will). Learn the lessons and go into the next game wiser and confidently.

If you have cards

You have the potential to make something out of nothing. Keep playing (living)

Your Boston is coming!

VOLUME 18

SEEDS PLANTED

How do you do something without an example; nobody is there to teach you and touch your emotions in such a manner that it's ingrained in you to do this when you are in this position.

Sometimes there are others that can stand in the place when circumstances have left a hole where integral parts of one's life are not present

So not having Pops around

Can lead to having Cops around

So, I give myself a Pound

That I didn't take that route

Losing Pops at 15 was 1 thing

But it's hard to be sad about losing something you hadn't seen in 8 years

it's hard to be scarred

By the loss of something you never had

We all got Fathers

What I wanted was a Dad

To school me and teach me

Discipline and Lead me

Not these Mom boyfriend losers

That couldn't even feed me

It's an internal anger
But no time for why me
75% of my childhood friends
Was raised without biological in the house either
Sure, some had stepdads, grandpas, or older brother's Some of us came up just sisters and single mothers
At some point, my subconscious had to decide
When I have a child repeat this cycle or be super committed
Committing to be good at something you never experienced is like teaching yourself Spanish in the middle of Italy
As Father's Day approaches, I realize I have tried to be the best Father I could be without a road map or experience
Yet, parenthood is an on-the-job training type of thing.
I did know that my children would not have the experience of absentee Fatherhood
As a Father I've come up short,

Made bad decisions, said, and done hurtful things, haven't had the words to say, spoiled kids to give them more than I had, etc. etc. etc.

But I was always present trying my best to be Dad.

It's my wish to one day see my children raise the bar and be even better parents to my grands.

JaVon, Dionna, James, and SaVonne Anderson

VOLUME 19

VIBRATIONAL CREATION

I'm so glad I didn't say anything to too many people when I was in such an emotional state

I'm so glad something inside me maybe embarrassment wouldn't let me speak more about it

I often hurt more for others whom I'm sure have had a similar experience

Many probably don't even know there is a name for this condition

Can't really talk about it because it's such a hard thing to explain unless you have experienced it

I had experienced it a few times ironically before I realized there was a litany of information on the internet explaining it

I'm so Glad those who did have the opportunity to show their true colors did

I'm so Glad I don't hold any hatred for the perpetrators or their minions

Whatever happens.... time heals all wounds

But you can use that time super wisely and level up Level Up your love for yourself.

Level Up your Love for self-improvement and self-awareness

Level Up and watch your circle shrink

I'm so glad I don't look like what I've been through I'm so glad my story is exactly what it is

I'm so glad that my son sees a vulnerable man when he sees his dad

"Thank You" by Me

Dad...

Thank you,

For all the times you made sure We were okay

For never going to sleep until I got home

For loving me when I didn't love myself

For being a helping hand when I didn't want to reach... Thank you.

An amazing man, and a greater father

We all have our flaws, but it's how you grow from them

Your flaws may be open, but they are also easier to fix. Your vulnerability for a man is admiring and amazing. Thank you.

For showing me that it's okay to be unapologetically me For helping me understand everything that glitters isn't gold For showing me that nothing in this world will come free For helping me become the person I am today. Thank You.

HAPPY FATHERS DAY.
JaVon Nasir Anderson

JaVon and the Doodler

VOLUME 20

YOU DON'T KNOW ME

Who Am I?

I'm not just a black entrepreneur

I'm a cat that struggled with having money for the first time

I'm not just a three-time divorcé

That might imply I'm afraid of commitment or run when the going got tough

Got a son and a daughter that I've never left. I am ever present in their lives.... like an expensive calculator - something they could always count on

Not just first in my family to graduate from college, also same kid that sold trees on campus

Guess I've been an entrepreneur

Kept it on the low

I was also president of a student organization

Same kid with Cancer never been healthier in my whole life Stopped putting poison in my body as a means of healing

Change my eating habits, walking more, mental health no longer taken for granted

Same ones you trust with your life can flip and have you feeling embarrassed

Who Am I?

To not exhibit self-love and self-care

Use to be afraid to fly and I wrote this in the air

In route to vacation in a place I never been

Coming up I was either in Newark or Chinquapin

Nowadays I'm quick to pop on a flight manifest

Took 40 years to realize affirmations, prayer, and spirituality is something that you got to develop for yourself. Going through a person, place or thing puts that person place or thing in touch with the creator not you

I'm all these things. Good and Bad

Same one Love me Today

Might hate me tomorrow

Most important that I know me

Most important that My opinion of me comes from a place of genuine Love

What's none of my business is what you think of me Sooner we all get that; sooner we all get free FROM EACH OTHER

VOLUME 21

TALK TO ME NICE

Hardest Thing about trying to be a nice person is:

A. Continuing to be nice to people that have made it clear they are taking advantage of your kindness

B. Continuing to be nice to people that have been unapologetic in their disrespectful treatment of you

C. Continuing to be nice to those that treat you in ways you have specifically asked them not to

D. None of the above.

Continuing to be nice to yourself as you recognize the need for and begin implementing boundaries around your "Niceness". It's challenging to be genuinely nice to yourself and not project those outwards to others. Same goes if I treat myself unlovingly, I am going to project that out too.

VOLUME 22

PARENTING 101

To be a child raised by a single parent because of a failed marriage, then the death of a parent and grow up to be a parent

of children raised by a single parent because of a failed marriage and then death of a parent is traumatic.

As a parent, I was imperfect under these circumstances; not from effort, desire, and attention to what I believed were the important things. In efforts to steer my children away from what hindered me in life, I may have left little space for them to express who they wanted to be. My Bad.

I always LOVED YOU.
In my mind I was doing what was best for you.

Parenting is hard.
Being a parent is hard.
We make the wrong decisions.
We grow.

We learn together.

That's what makes us family.

Our individual circumstances.

The challenges and specific mountains we climb together. Creates the glue to hold us together.

Javon, James and SaVonne Anderson

VOLUME 23

FUNERAL ARRANGEMENTS

For years I had dreams for my funeral to be fully packed with people.

See if my funeral was going to be crowded with hundreds of people that would show how good of a person I was. How valuable I was as a man. Yes, we want our legacy to be one of substance. Yet while I am here, I should be living a life that I am enjoying so that I am happy with myself. This made me realize I was so IN LOVE with what others think about me that even in death one of my concerns is how people would show up for me. Though the thought is about the future, how easily those dreams can dictate (be no confrontational and a doormat) in hopes that this will garner someone's allegiance and commitment to me. How foolish. I had to fall out of LOVE with people's perception of me and fall in LOVE for the first time with my LOVE for me. Not based on my possessions, accomplishments, people I knew, the way I dressed, or anything else external. Nor unloving myself because of mistakes I made, lies I told, bad choices I made, unfulfilled promises, or any of my hundreds of other shortcomings. So, I now would rather live that life for myself and if there are 10 people at my funeral services I would rather it be ten people who TRULY Love and Care about me, not hundreds of distant people many that may be a little happy that I am gone.

I had to learn to LOVE myself unconditionally. I had loved so many others unconditionally (putting up with poor treatment of myself at my own expense) for years. Loving oneself isn't huffed up and conceited but rather humble and grounded. One must know one's self worth and have boundaries and deal breakers connected to that worth. If someone breaks a boundary they can be told once about the issue if this is someone you want to be in your life or the extent of the offense. In some cases, once may be enough. In other instances, you may want to provide an opportunity for repair and receive a genuine effort from the other party at remorse and reconciliation

VOLUME 24

CHEMOTHERAPY IS LIKE ETHER

Chemotherapy is like Ether. It gets in your soul.

In essence, it's deciding to poison yourself for the possible greater good. The conversation with yourself kind of goes I want to live longer so to do so I may have to expose myself to loss of hair, loss of appetite, possible volcanic diarrhea, constipation, nausea, loss of sexual appetite, or ability, weight loss, nail discoloration, kidney failure, lung failure, blood clots, insomnia, and in rare cases death.

I'm a Soul Survivor.
What are the blessings of Cancer?

When you get an incurable diagnosis, life gets real serious real quick. Zero to One Hundred real quick.

What do I need to get in order?
Final Conversations.
Giving my final wishes.
Prepping for what may be inevitable.

Would you rather have a sudden death Or here today and gone tomorrow? Unexpected premature death or be fully aware and see the possibility on the horizon?

I don't know how many of us, especially under 60 prepare for death: which is guaranteed to each of us. If I knew I was getting laid off in a month, I would spend this present paycheck a little differently than if I do now.

VOLUME 25

MONEY NOT THE ANSWER

Sometimes it's the process one goes through to be better with how you use money. That's the blessing of not having

money. Sometimes we have enough dollars, but not enough sense.

Financial Literacy is the key to financial freedom. You can't make any stance for justice or freedom if you are financially obligated and under someone else paying you to survive the next two weeks.

Ask Yourself: How many weeks could I live without a paycheck from my current employer?

Anything that has to do with something outside of self is not the answer.

Not people, not possessions, not even family.

All these things can be heightened once we start to practice experiencing the answer.

SELF LOVE IS THE ANSWER

VOLUME 26

A FACE FULL OF TEARS

I cried today.
I cried last week.

I cry often.

I smiled today.
I laughed last week.
I laugh and smile often.

Such is Life.
Balance is Life.

I smile and laugh when I think of how I overcame the moments of wiping a face full of tears.

VOLUME 27

IF I DIE TODAY

No one knows.

The full story of my life.

I mean, especially like all the lows.

Some know this and some know that but sometimes things happen that just seem so unbelievable.

It's hard to fix your mouth to share it with someone else

God forbid, you take the chance of sharing, and that trusted person can't wrap their head around it to believe what you just shared. I mean some experiences are so unbelievable that people may think you are either lying or exaggerating, or they just don't know what to do, and in turn, do nothing.

That has been my experience on occasion, so I stopped expecting support, empathy, or tender care in those tough times.

I started looking at that man in the mirror for validation. Trying to live out this SELF CARE, SELF LOVE, SEMI VEGAN, YOGA, AND MEDITATION VIBE.

So, I know the whole story, and the more I realize who is most important, the more I can provide myself with support, empathy, and tender care. It's ok to have this from external sources, but if you don't have it in you, one is at the mercy of those outside sources providing it for you.

Define and Provide Self Care for Yourself.

VOLUME 28

CANCER - STILL MY FRIEND

Never wanted you.
Never thought I'd meet you.

No one in my family had been introduced to you.
So never did I think I would have an encounter with you. Just as life does, we had an impromptu introduction in 2015. Doctors "DIAGNOSED" me with having you.

First thoughts of Fear: I don't want this, and death consumed me.
Then thoughts of overcoming, beating all the odds, and trusting in the doctors began to flourish.

Finally, and more lasting have been thoughts of Self Care, Self-Reliance, and Self Reflection and Assurance.

I'm treating my health situation with My Self Love Diet. Eating like a Vegetarian, Peace over Toxicity, Solitude over Fitting In, Yoga/Meditation over Gossip/Anxiety, Peace Over Everything.

I believe stress and unresolved trauma in my life had as much to do with my diagnosis as anything.

So, no more Pharmaceuticals.

No More activities of Self Hate.

No more enabling.

No more sharing where I'm unappreciated.

No more playing the COVID game and wearing a mask.

I'm working to get to know myself and healing in the process. Physically, Mentally and Emotionally.

Funny how this friend Cancer came along into this sick vessel with many friends and as I heal, my circle of trust gets smaller and smaller.

Seems like Cancer really came to improve my life. I no longer move to impress people. If my life inspires, cool. If my life makes you uncomfortable, cool.

Friends, Family, Foe, or Fan, I LOVE YOU. As I heal, my test results make it harder and harder for the doctors to stand behind their diagnosis.

VOLUME 29

BREATHE AGAIN

I was just trying to breathe!!

That day came and hit me like a ton of bricks.
I wasn't on my therapist's couch when it happened, but it was surely an outgrowth of those sessions

I WAS SO BROKEN THAT I HAD BECOME NEEDY OF THINGS: OUTSIDE OF ME TO COMPLETE ME.

*THINGS = possessions, friends, admiration, and women.

All the things society said represented success.
My subconscious desire to please society was so ingrained that it was like breathing to me. Something I didn't have to think about doing but when it stopped, I felt like I was dying.

This became most apparent in my marital life. Three wives and three divorces. I'm a good dude. Why is this happening to me over and over? I was just trying to breathe. That unchecked societal box didn't sit well with me. As a result, I continued to try to check it. Whenever you make "want" decisions from a place of "need", you are sure to sell yourself short.

I am starting to breathe on my own now. Falling in love with me was the key to my breath control the whole time. Putting my breath in the hands of others was giving others control of my life. I must THINK about this breathing seriously. If not, the old breathing pattern is sure to resurface.

VOLUME 30

FEAR FACTOR

We know there is better than this, but fear has us staying here. If this is the best, we will be committed to fear of fear.

Oh, to be blessed with the love from another, that you love just as much!

Those times we refer to as the honeymoon period are filled with highs that years later can carry us through some substantial lows.

That honeymoon period is just the first quarter of the game.

We can keep the game close and make some real decisions at halftime.

The major decision is how vulnerable, and intimate are we willing to be with each other? For example, by halftime, we know many of our opponents' strengths, weaknesses, tendencies, comfort zones, etc. I specifically used the word opponent because we're going to have to decide in the locker room if we will leave as a united team, committed to like goals and means of attainment; or opponents fighting for a great relationship through unhealed traumas and triggers that don't allow or minimally foster the relationship we see for ourselves.

You may be standing in your own way.

Yelling over yourself at the person you are in a relationship with.

We know there is better than this.
We've experienced it.
If only briefly.
Consider giving up being good individual players.
While becoming a great team
You Scared? Or Are You Scarred?

VOLUME 31

DENVER

Never thought of Denver as a bucket list place to visit. Yet, I had some of my greatest times during the pandemic in Denver, Colorado. Nature and city life are just stepping away from each other and the beauty of the city is ever so inviting.

It was in these experiences that I saw the potential in truly loving someone. As I stand in raging waters, smack in the middle of the city in Confluence Park, I marveled at how rocks seemed to have been shaped by the water. This wasn't an overnight process, but a gentle one over time. Reminded me of how over time two souls gently massage each other into coexisting in a way that is beneficial to both parties.

The water doesn't get impatient with the process and the rock doesn't fight against being altered for the greater good.

The creator has a way of instructing us through nature. The greatest beauty was that the coexistence was there not for the rocks or the water, but the creator had it here for us to enjoy. Nature is always there for our enjoyment and instruction. I'm forever grateful for my experience in Confluence Park, – Denver, CO.

VOLUME 32

IMAGINATION

Never imagined being divorced three times.

Never imagined I would be diagnosed with Multiple Myeloma.

Never imagined I would be working for myself for more than half my employment life.

Never imagined I would be single.

Never imagined I would need hip replacement surgery.

Never imagined I would be practicing yoga.

Never imagined I would be questioning the Bible.

Never imagined I would be in therapy (all these years).

Never imagined I would have to hold myself down.

Never imagined I needed to be healed from my inner brokenness...

Never realized how lonely you can be surrounded by many people, and how complete you can feel with just yourself.

Doodles Of a Survivor: My Journey To James

VOLUME 33

YOUR PEOPLES

Before you introduce a person to your people, you better vet that person.

An unvetted demon let loose on your people, can write a secret narrative right beneath your nose.

As your people and the person have this twisted perspective,

whilst smiling in your face the whole time.

When a person slips and exposes themselves to you and you go to your people for support,

It's like changing faces. They can't hear you through the false narrative the person has been feeding them behind your back for months, if not years. In one swoop you lose your personality and your people.

I spent exorbitant amounts of time focused on the secret sins of the person until one day it hit me…

If I had people; no person could infiltrate that.

Maybe the person was sent to expose the people.

PERFECT

VOLUME 34

UNBREAKABLE

Peshine Ave School Circa 1983

5th-grade student

Excellent Grades.

Cool kid but still the teacher's pet.

So much so Mr. Ferugio would give me time out of class.

Mr. Ferugio was responsible for teacher supplies (an additional responsibility I'm sure for which he was compensated).

Not only did Mr. Ferugio take care of this responsibility during the time he was supposed to be teaching, but he also took a few other selected students and me with him as assistants (unpaid I might add - sound familiar?). This went on for months equaling many hours of education time where the selected assistants weren't learning. And the other students weren't left behind in the classroom without a teacher. One of the teachers in an adjacent classroom was responsible for "overseeing" the unattended students making sure they weren't being rambunctious.

The seed was planted in the unselected students to behave in the teacher's absence so that they might be "selected" next time.

I was selected every time and picked up on the process quickly. This was at least 20% of my 5th grade year. It wasn't until 6th grade, when I was in Mr. Ferugio's friend's class, that I realized this was a group effort. See, in 6th grade I was "promoted". I was now being taken out of class and sent to the supply room to manage the other selected students ...by myself.

I thought I was getting over. It wasn't until I was an adult that I realized Mr. Ferugio was the one getting over all the time. There had to be a lot of people who saw, acted like they didn't see, or maybe didn't care about educating us.

I still see many of my classmates from those days. They're a whole lot of successful people despite our miseducation. I'm proud of you all

TRUE STORY ALL FACTS

PS-after missing out on all that class time (working), I was rewarded by being submitted and selected to attend University Junior High Gifted and Talented Program. A former A+ student began to fail as I was unprepared for this new educational rigor. Thank God, I was able to not only catch up academically but became the first college graduate in my family.

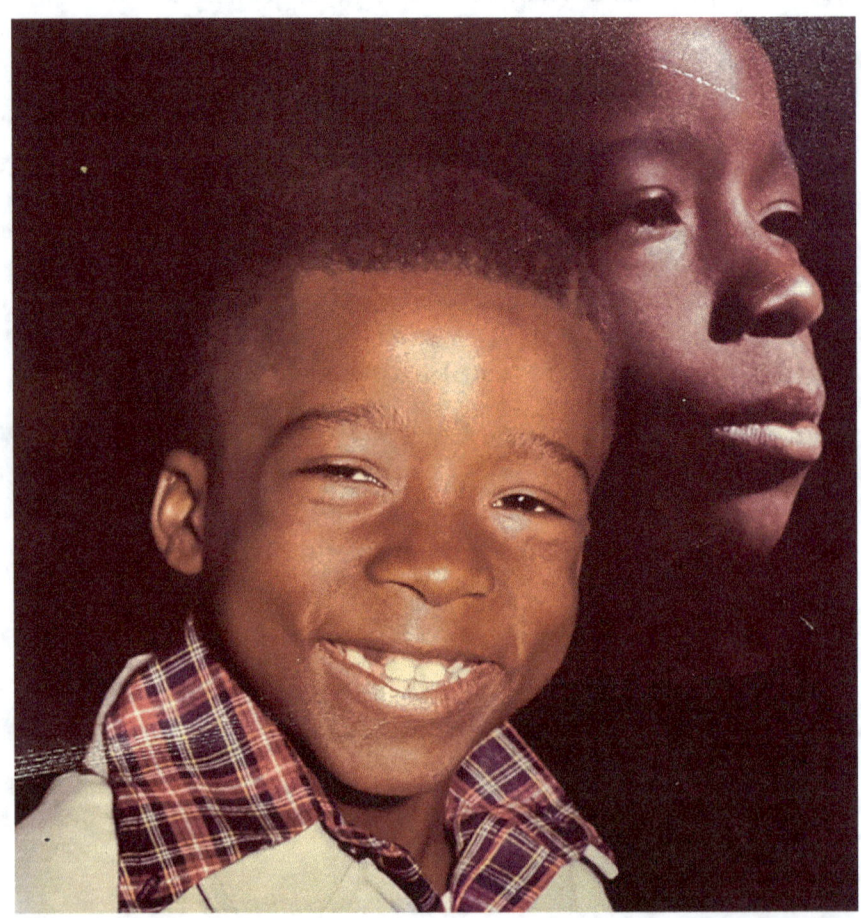

VOLUME 35

HANDLEBARS

Being in love is like riding a bike.

Learning to ride a bike is very synonymous with life.

It takes effort, courage, consistency, and persistence to learn to ride a bike. All the same skills we need to develop for success in life.

With repetition, we get better and better at it. I see it synonymous with seeing a cyclist pop a wheelie for half a block…that's us killing it in life. As beautiful as that is, it's mainly an activity focused on the individual.

To include another in "this activity/your life", is like letting the handlebars go and trusting another to have some control over your ride/life.

Just like when you first let the handlebars go and rode "no hands", we are barely letting go and ready to take hold of the handlebars again as soon as we feel the least bit uncomfortable.

Letting go of the handlebars and having that confidence honored and protected by the ones assigned is love. Having that trust abused or taken for granted is a love lesson, not a sign to never do it again.

I pray we all get to experience riding no hands even if only for a little while.

Afterthought- you will charge some people with controlling your handlebars. They will fail your trust and you may crash. Get up and ride again. You can miss out on the greatest love opportunity holding onto the handlebars.

VOLUME 36

SELFISH

We Are Never Taught to BE SELFISH Getting the listed Selves in order makes interactions with others better.

Self-Love
Self Help
Self-Development
Self Sufficient
Self-Reliant
Self-Determination
Self-Employed
Self-Protective
Self-Motivated
Self-Care
Self-Reflective
Take the time to get all of yourselves in order.

VOLUME 37

BLIND SPOTS-HANDLEBARS 2

A relationship is like driving a car with no rear-view mirrors. You must trust that you have chosen the right co-pilot.

You must trust your co-pilot has your best interest, as they give input on what's coming up on the sides of you.

If you lack trust and decrease your concentration, second-guess your co-pilot, and try to look, there's a great chance of an accident.

Yet, even worse, if you look and don't crash, one is more comfortable looking the next time and not trusting your partner.

The downside to looking yourself, and not taking any warnings or direction from your partner, is that they soon feel unnecessary and ignored.

Sure, you can look at yourself and essentially ride alone safely in the space that you've created.

In addition, think about how much more relaxed you can be if you trusted that your co-pilot understands that giving poor direction could injure you both.

In our own safety we can control all the outcomes and become slaves to our fears. Trusting your co-pilot to show you some blind spots that you can't see on your own creates an environment where trust, safety, and love is navigated by communication and not fear.

The Worst thing you can do is get behind the wheel, ignore your co-pilot and crash…then look at your co-pilot as the problem.

Communication, Cooperation, and Trust…

When most of us get to a certain age, we need help with our vision.

We rarely make it through a full day without our help (glasses, contact lenses, etc.) But nevertheless, we're living like we have total 20/20 vision over our existence. I've been on both sides.

Neither will get you the desired result of a healthy relationship.

I hear you all… "but I can't trust this joker" … sounds like a relationship you shouldn't be in anyway.

We lose too many relationships because we're unable to hear someone tell us about our blind spots.

VOLUME 38

PANDEMIC THOUGHTS

The greatest day of my life was when I developed a willingness to see things differently than I had been programmed to.

Generally, and subconsciously people don't like hearing good things.

We're addicted to bad news and negativity. Bad news travels fast. The news of me having cancer, I'm sure came off more lips than, "hey this kid was raised by a single Mom, in Newark, NJ, graduated from college, created a business out of his teenage hobby, and has been successfully operating it for over 15 years.

It's Natural to have pain and troubles.

It's unnatural to be suffering because of pain and troubles.

Pain and troubles will come, but I refuse to willingly suffer because of them.

Break the programming.

It's ok to fail. It's the reaction to the failure that causes problems.

Change Your Reaction

No one has ever hurt me in my entire life!!!!

My response to what they may have done hurt me.

I only began to live when I was told I was going to die.

Irony is we are all born dying, so best get to living.

VOLUME 39

SELF LOVE / ALGORITHMS

An **algorithm is a series of instructions telling a computer how to transform a set of facts about the world into useful information**. The facts are data, and the useful information is knowledge for people, instructions for machines, or input for yet another algorithm.

Usually, we think of algorithms in the sense of social media and who is seeing or not seeing my posts. Yet, the brain is running algorithms that we input the "facts" into every day. The facts that we input are often flawed and based on our opinions, experiences, and what society or one's family of origin has fed you.

The computer can't think. You can.

Become an author of your thoughts.

Might discover you've been running an algorithm that doesn't support your self-love.

Doodles Of a Survivor: My Journey To James

VOLUME 40

SOLEIL

Anticipated lunch with my first born.

Monumental because we have begun healing our fractured relationship.

I stand on the corner waiting for her to arrive at the restaurant, passing time on my phone.

I look up and she has snuck up on me. Thirty feet away and as our eyes meet, she displays that crooked grin that precedes her full-on smile. Within the 30 feet that she had to walk to get to me, I had so many thoughts: "damn, she looks just like Asia. Look how grown up my little baby has gotten. It's nice to see her smiling. She looks really happy." Because of the difficulty in our relationship, I didn't fully celebrate with her some major accomplishments she had in the past 18 months, so I'm always happy to see her happy despite our discomfort.

We sat and made small talk for a few minutes. Although we had spent time together prior to this meeting, the mood felt significantly lighter. Just as I had that thought, I made a comment about her statement in a previous text conversation that she was going to be moving in a couple months. We didn't talk about it much, but I decided to circle back to it to get the deets. I was low key fishing to see if she was moving in with her long-time boyfriend.

She shocked me with another accomplishment. She had applied and been selected to live in a new entrepreneur business hub that includes on site income-based housing in newly built apartments, and a storefront for your business on the lower level. Just as I was thinking of not celebrating some significant achievements, up close I get the opportunity live and in person to celebrate with her in the moment. Felt like our first adult connected parent/child occasion. It was such great news, a great opportunity. I know she's deserving.

Before I could get up to hug her, she slips a paper out of her purse folded up and slides it to me. I'm thinking she is showing me some check stub for her services for an ungodly amount. As soon as I felt the texture of the paper my mind shifted. I didn't want to jump the gun, so I looked at her. There it was: her crooked grin. I wasn't sure if it was a confirmation look, so I said, "this paper feels very specific to one thing". She simply shook her head, kind of confirming without saying a word, motioning for me to look…

What I anticipated was having lunch with my daughter and continuing to lay the foundations for healing our relationship.

I left feeling that the foundation didn't have to be rebuilt but dusted off and altered, because it's still there.

I left feeling so proud of this young lady, knowing all the doors she has kicked down, and strides she has made as a young black female entrepreneur.

I left feeling like the door that we both had been opening slowly, was wide open now.

I left knowing that I have the skill to differentiate sonogram paper from others!!!!

MY BABY IS HAVING A BABY!!

SaVONNE DaSAWNDRA ANDERSON is going to be a MOM.

I was so happy for my daughter, to be a part of this moment, and looking forward to all the moments in this pregnancy and child rearing. I spent a lot of time telling her how proud of her I was. I let her know how I believe the more mature we are as parents, the better job we can do as parents and not societal norm programmers. I confessed to being guilty of parenting her siblings and her like this often. I encouraged them to do better than I did.

We had a good time, a connected time, and as I drove home engulfed in love, joy, and happiness looking forward to babysitting, a tear came to my eye with the realization…" this little joker will NOT be calling me GRANDPA".

In 2015 when doctors diagnosed me with multiple myeloma, I was afraid I would continue the generational curse in my family, of parents never meeting their grandchildren because of untimely deaths. I think I cried today because I'm going to break it.

James E. Anderson Jr

James and SaVonne Anderson

VOLUME 41

PROTECTING MY PEACE

It's ok to be disappointed by another's behavior. It's the reaction to the disappointment that causes problems. If I have zero control over anyone else's behavior, why put my faith in it?? People are free to do whatever they choose and that will or may never be in 100% agreement with my thoughts. To protect my peace, I choose to work hard to be in control of my peace. I believe true peace comes from an unshakable ability to always respond and never react.

Wild animals react.

You're a human who can respond.

You're a human who can respond in ways that honor and protect your peace. You're a human who can choose how and to what you will respond.

Animal/knee jerk reactions from humans often lead to apologies and forgiveness on the lightest end, with death and imprisonment as more serious consequences of these types of reactions.

Change your reaction!

Take your power back!

Choose how you will respond!

Practice responding and not reacting!

I hear some of you now… "WHAT AM I SUPPOSED TO DO IF SOMEONE HURTS ME"

A very true and seemingly insensitive statement that later served as a huge aha moment for me was hearing for the first time:

No one has ever hurt YOU in your entire life!

Your response to what they did hurt you.

Choose to respond differently if it's about your peace

My mind was initially hurt, then blown, and finally Freed.

I now understand I have all control over how I respond to anyone's behavior. That response will always, foremost, protect my peace.

VOLUME 42

FALL SEMESTER 1990

Rutgers Newark circa 1990 doing Work-Study at the gym with my roommate John Capers.

As a group of young ladies walk into the gym

I leaned over with my 19-year-old self and said

"John, I'm going to marry that girl right there".

I didn't even know her name but was committing my life to her.

Seems crazy but by Dec 2, 1992

She was my girlfriend.

Then my co-parent and fiancé in 1994.

And on July 27, 1997, the prediction was official.

And Asia Davis became my wife.

We didn't maintain the fairy tale beginning and have a long successful marriage.

We even expressed hatred instead of love towards each other for a time.

Yet, we forgave and got back to love and co-parenting before you departed physically.

We are always connected.

Divorce couldn't split the two children we created from being ours.

Asia Davis Anderson

AKA

Fall Semester 1990

SaVonne, Asia Davis-Anderson, James, and JaVon Anderson

IN CLOSING

I keep writing more doodles as life keeps unveiling itself to me. I credit a loose dedication to the practices of mindfulness, meditation, yoga, and opening my mind to other spiritual practices with inspiration. Not to mention the encouragement I receive when someone tells me they were inspired by one of my doodles. I write and share as an exercise in vulnerability, humility, and self-acceptance. Accepting myself is the biggest part as I have learned, not just in theory, that self-acceptance: knowing my own strengths, weaknesses, and loving them all, even the ones I'm working to improve, is central to accepting and loving others. It's the love and connection with other imperfect souls that I've always unconsciously craved. I needed life to teach me that everything I crave, may not be meant for my consumption.

These doodles help me to look at my life experiences differently: to view people differently; in a way that empowers me. I hope they help others experience their real power for the first time or realize they can go back and get it if they handed it over to someone or something else.

So, stay tuned for more doodles to come. As I accept myself more, cultivate my strengths and weaknesses, and undergo more aha moments, I invite you in to share in this journey of a survivor, as I creatively and humbly share snippets of my life thoughts and experiences.

You are invited into my life's construction site, as I work myself into the James that the creator sees when she sees me. I'm working my way back to the James who was lost trying to honor societal norms and bogus beliefs. On this site, I'm deconstructing many of the truths I've inherited from family or society that do not serve me or my beliefs. Simultaneously, I am building and developing my own truths and beliefs that I get to choose and abide by.

An outgrowth from the doodles has been the Statement Teez development, which can be found on https://immateez.com. These statements are often inspired by the same process that produces the doodles.

Please go to https://immateez.com. I hope you're inspired to support the movement.

Sign up for the newsletter to keep abreast of all things @immateez.

www.ingramcontent.com/pod-product-compliance
Lightning Source LLC
Chambersburg PA
CBHW071503070526
44578CB00001B/424